Scott of the ANTARCTIC

Evelyn Dowdeswell, Julian Dowdeswell,
and Angela Seddon

Heinemann
LIBRARY

Chicago, Illinois

www.capstonepub.com
Visit our website to find out more information about Heinemann-Raintree books.

To order:
☎ Phone 888-454-2279
💻 Visit www.capstonepub.com
to browse our catalog and order online.

Edited by Dan Nunn and Sian Smith
Designed by Richard Parker
Picture research by Hannah Taylor
Production by Alison Parsons

Originated by Capstone Global Library Ltd
Printed and bound in China by South China Printing Company Ltd

4971 8389 10/12

15 14 13 12 11
10 9 8 7 6 5 4 3 2 1

Library of Congress Cataloging-in-Publication Data
Dowdeswell, Evelyn.
  Scott of the Antarctic / Evelyn Dowdeswell, Julian Dowdeswell, and Angela Seddon. p.cm.
  Includes bibliographical references and index.
  ISBN 978-1-4329-6890-8 (hb)—ISBN 978-1-4329-6891-5 (pb) 1. Scott, Robert Falcon, 1868-1912. 2. British Antarctic ("Terra Nova") Expedition (1910-1913) 3. Antarctica—Discovery and exploration—British. I. Dowdeswell, J. A. II. Seddon, Angela. III. Title.
  G8501910 .D68 2013
  919.8'9—dc23   2011037936

Acknowledgments
We would like to thank the following for permission to reproduce images: © Corbis p. 28 (Ann Hawthorne); © Julian Dowdeswell pp. 5, 22 (both), 29; © Scott Polar Research Institute, University of Cambridge pp. 4, 6, 7, 10, 11, 12, 13, 14 (main), 14 (inset), 15, 16, 17, 19, 20, 21, 23, 24, 25, 26, 27 (main), 27 (inset); Shutterstock p. 8 (©Photo dynamic); USGS p. 9. Background design features reproduced with permission of Shutterstock: background 1 (©Tyler Olson); background 2 (©Similaun Man); background 3 (©April Cat).

Cover photographs of Captain Scott and the Antarctic Expedition group reproduced with permission of ©Scott Polar Research Institute, University of Cambridge, England. Background cover image reproduced with permission of Shutterstock (©Similaun Man).

We would like to thank Lucy Martin and Louise Galpine for their invaluable help in the preparation of this book.

Contents

Some words are shown in bold, **like this**.
You can find out what they mean by looking
in the glossary on page 31.

Who Was Captain Scott?

In 1911, two groups of men set off to reach the **South Pole** for the first time. Roald Amundsen arrived there first. But Robert Falcon Scott's heroic adventure and death will also always be remembered.

This photograph shows Captain Scott standing next to his sled.

The South Pole is the most **southern** place in the world. It is roughly in the middle of the continent of **Antarctica**. At the South Pole it is dark all the time in winter and light all summer.

Antarctica

Antarctica is so cold that there are no trees anywhere on the continent.

Early Years

Robert Falcon Scott was born near Plymouth, England, on June 6, 1868. He had a brother and four sisters. In school, Robert studied hard. He wanted to join the **navy** like two of his uncles.

Robert grew up in a big house in the country.

Robert joined the navy when he was just 13 years old!

After school, Robert joined the British Royal Navy. Learning to sail ships was hard work, but Robert did well. He became Captain Scott when he was chosen to lead **expeditions** to the **Antarctic** in 1901 and 1910.

The Unknown Antarctic

The **Antarctic** is the coldest place on Earth. It is almost completely covered with very thick ice and is surrounded by a cold ocean. Penguins and seals live there.

Penguins are among the few animals that live in Antarctica.

Captain Scott wanted to be the first person to reach the **South Pole**. He also wanted to study the Antarctic. Nobody knew much about **Antarctica** 100 years ago.

Today, there are buildings at the South Pole. But 100 years ago, no one had ever been there!

Sailing to the Antarctic

On his first trip to the **Antarctic**, in 1901, Captain Scott and his crew traveled in a wooden sailing ship called the *Discovery*. The *Discovery* had to be big enough to carry everything the 47 people and 23 dogs needed.

The *Discovery* had to be very strong to sail through sea ice.

Captain Scott's second ship, the *Terra Nova*, had a special **stable** for the **expedition** ponies.

Captain Scott had to take food, fuel, medicine, and other supplies for life in the Antarctic with him. He also took scientific equipment, books, and even a piano! On his second trip, in 1910, he took ponies and motorized sleds as well.

Life in the Antarctic

When the **expedition** members arrived in the **Antarctic**, they had to build a hut to live in. They also needed somewhere for the animals to stay.

The hut was warm and snug against the strong wind and cold Antarctic night.

Can you see some of the things that Captain Scott took with him to the Antarctic?

As leader of the expedition, Captain Scott had his own area in the hut. It was here that he planned the exploration of the Antarctic and the team's scientific work.

These photos show the bunk beds and kitchen in Captain Scott's **Antarctic** hut.

Other members of the **expedition** slept in bunk beds. Captain Scott's men used boxes of supplies to make walls inside the hut. There was also a kitchen where meals were prepared.

Everyone stayed inside during the long winter months, keeping warm around the stove. When they finished their work, they wrote diaries, painted pictures, and sang songs.

Here, two of Captain Scott's men are cooking food for the ponies and keeping warm at the same time!

Traveling on the Ice

When spring came, Captain Scott and his men practiced pulling their sleds using skis, **snowshoes**, dogs, and ponies. They also had motorized sleds on the second trip, but the sleds broke down in the very cold weather.

The motorized sleds ran on tracks, similar to a tank.

When they were ready, Captain Scott and his men set out for the **South Pole**. They pulled sleds loaded with tents, food, and fuel, helped by ponies and dogs. Traveling over the soft snow was very hard work.

The sleds were very heavy. Each one weighed more than 220 pounds (100 kilograms). That is like pulling 220 bags of sugar!

Reaching the South Pole

On his first **expedition**, Captain Scott had walked closer to the **South Pole** than anyone else at that time. He eventually reached the South Pole on January 17, 1912, on his second trip.

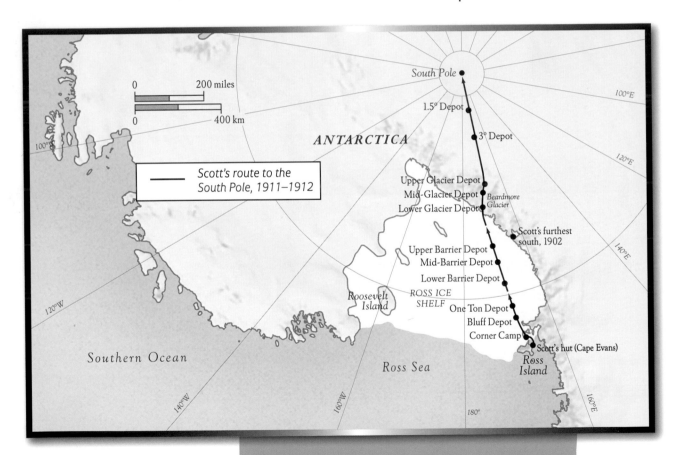

Depots of food were left for the return trip.

Doctor Wilson. | Captain Scott. | Petty Officer Evans. | Captain Oates. | Lieut: Bowers.

A number of men helped carry supplies on the trip, but only five went all the way to the South Pole.

It took Captain Scott and his four **companions** 78 days to travel the 900 miles (1,450 kilometers) from their hut to the South Pole. When they got there, they were cold, hungry, and very tired.

Captain Scott and his men had wanted to be the first people to reach the **South Pole**. However, when they got there, they were disappointed to find out that a Norwegian explorer, Roald Amundsen, had gotten there a month before.

Amundsen's team left a tent and letters for Captain Scott at the South Pole.

The next spring, members of Captain Scott's team built a **cairn** of snow over the place where he died.

The journey back from the South Pole was very long, and the cold days of fall were coming. Captain Scott and his four **companions** never arrived back at their hut. They died of cold and lack of food on their way back.

Remembering Captain Scott

When the news came back that Captain Scott and his men had reached the **South Pole**, their story became known around the world. The Scott Polar Research Institute in Cambridge, England, was set up to remember their bravery and achievements in the cold **Antarctic**.

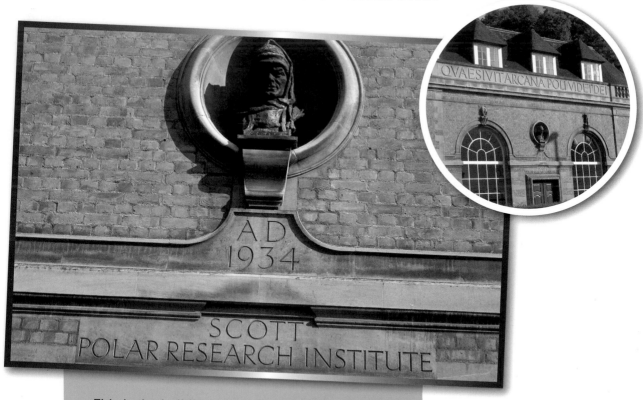

This is the building of the Scott Polar Research Institute in Cambridge, England.

The Scott Polar Research Institute's museum has scientific displays about the Antarctic and the **ice sheet** that covers it. It also has letters, diaries, and other objects from Captain Scott's **expeditions** there.

These goggles, gloves, and **balaclava** were worn by Captain Scott and his men in the Antarctic.

Paintings and Photographs

We can find out more about Captain Scott, his **companions**, and the **Antarctic** by looking at paintings and photographs. Edward Wilson was a scientist and artist who went on the **South Pole** journey with Captain Scott.

In this photograph, Edward Wilson can be seen working on a painting in the expedition hut.

The large painting shows people camping in a **blizzard**. Wilson also liked to paint pictures of penguins.

Expedition members like Wilson had plenty of time to paint, especially in the winter when they had to stay in the hut because it was dark all the time and also very cold. These are two of his paintings.

A photographer, Herbert Ponting, also went with Captain Scott to the **Antarctic**. He took many photographs of the trip. Here is a photograph of the members of Captain Scott's **expedition**.

Can you see the hats, gloves, and boots that Captain Scott and his men used to keep out the cold?

Ponting's photographs showed people what the Antarctic was like. The photograph on the right shows an ice cave, with the ship *Terra Nova* in the background.

The smaller photograph shows Herbert Ponting standing next to his camera.

The Antarctic Today

People still explore the **Antarctic** today. Some are trying to learn more about the land and weather, as well as the animals that live there. Others are trying to set records.

In 1994, Liv Arnesen became the first woman to ski alone and unsupported to the South Pole.

Today's Antarctic scientists are able to use modern equipment to help them with their work.

Captain Scott's team thought that scientific discoveries were just as important as reaching the **South Pole**. Today, scientists study ice in **Antarctica** to learn about Earth's **climate**. Their discoveries may help us protect Earth in the future.

Captain Scott Timeline

June 6, 1868	Robert Falcon Scott is born
July 1881	Robert joins the British Royal **Navy**
July 1901	Captain Scott leads his first British **Antarctic Expedition** on the *Discovery*
January 1902	Captain Scott crosses the Southern Ocean and sees **Antarctica** for the first time
December 1902	Captain Scott sets the record for going the farthest south
September 1908	Robert Scott marries Kathleen Bruce
June 1910	Captain Scott leaves Great Britain on his second journey to the Antarctic, aboard the *Terra Nova*
November 1, 1911	Captain Scott sets out from his hut at Cape Evans toward the **South Pole**
January 17, 1912	Captain Scott reaches the South Pole
March 29, 1912	The last entry is made in Captain Scott's diary, making it the probable date of his death

Glossary

Antarctic south polar region

Antarctica very cold continent located around the South Pole

balaclava knit hat that covers the head and neck, and which has a hole for the eyes

blizzard storm with wind and blowing snow

cairn human-made heap or pile of snow or stones

climate usual weather in a place

companion someone who spends a lot of time with another person

depot place where supplies are stored

expedition journey that is taken by a person or group of people to little-known places

ice sheet thick ice that covers a large area

navy part of a country's armed forces that works at sea

snowshoe platform shaped like a tennis racket that can be attached to a shoe. Snowshoes are used to help people walk across snow without sinking.

South Pole place that is as far south as you can go

southern in the direction of the south

stable building that animals are kept in

Find Out More

Books

Gogerly, Liz. *Amundsen and Scott's Race to the South Pole* (Great Journeys Across Earth). Chicago: Heinemann Library, 2008.

Llanas, Sheila Griffin. *Who Reached the South Pole First?* (Fact Finders). Mankato, Minn.: Capstone, 2011.

Markle, Sandra. *Animals Robert Scott Saw: An Adventure in Antarctica*. San Francisco: Chronicle, 2008.

Web site

www.amnh.org/exhibitions/race

This web site offers maps, photos, and more that explore Scott's journey.

Index

Mc

rou

P
C